THE DISCOVERY
OF
THE ESSENE GOSPEL OF PEACE

To the memory of John XXIII—
In his wise compassion
He was "Il Papa" to millions.
In his creative thought
He was the harbinger of a new age.
In his heart
He was an Essene.

THE DISCOVERY
OF
THE ESSENE GOSPEL OF PEACE
THE ESSENES AND THE VATICAN

by

EDMOND BORDEAUX SZEKELY

MCMLXXVII
INTERNATIONAL BIOGENIC SOCIETY

SOME BOOKS BY EDMOND BORDEAUX SZEKELY

THE ESSENE WAY—BIOGENIC LIVING
THE ESSENE GOSPEL OF PEACE, BOOK ONE
BOOK TWO, THE UNKNOWN BOOKS OF THE ESSENES
BOOK THREE, LOST SCROLLS OF THE ESSENE BROTHERHOOD
BOOK FOUR, THE TEACHINGS OF THE ELECT
THE DISCOVERY OF THE ESSENE GOSPEL: The Essenes & the Vatican
SEARCH FOR THE AGELESS, in Three Volumes
THE ESSENE BOOK OF CREATION
THE ESSENE JESUS
THE ESSENE BOOK OF ASHA
THE ZEND AVESTA OF ZARATHUSTRA
ARCHEOSOPHY, A NEW SCIENCE
THE ESSENE ORIGINS OF CHRISTIANITY
TEACHINGS OF THE ESSENES FROM ENOCH TO THE DEAD SEA SCROLLS
THE ESSENES, BY JOSEPHUS AND HIS CONTEMPORARIES
THE ESSENE TEACHINGS OF ZARATHUSTRA
THE ESSENE SCIENCE OF LIFE
THE ESSENE CODE OF LIFE
THE ESSENE SCIENCE OF FASTING AND THE ART OF SOBRIETY
ESSENE COMMUNIONS WITH THE INFINITE
THE FIRST ESSENE
COSMOTHERAPY OF THE ESSENES
THE LIVING BUDDHA
TOWARD THE CONQUEST OF THE INNER COSMOS
JOURNEY THROUGH A THOUSAND MEDITATIONS
FATHER, GIVE US ANOTHER CHANCE
THE ECOLOGICAL HEALTH GARDEN, THE BOOK OF SURVIVAL
THE TENDER TOUCH: BIOGENIC FULFILLMENT
MAN IN THE COSMIC OCEAN
THE DIALECTICAL METHOD OF THINKING
THE EVOLUTION OF HUMAN THOUGHT
THE GREATNESS IN THE SMALLNESS
THE SOUL OF ANCIENT MEXICO
THE NEW FIRE
DEATH OF THE NEW WORLD
ANCIENT AMERICA: PARADISE LOST
PILGRIM OF THE HIMALAYAS
MESSENGERS FROM ANCIENT CIVILIZATIONS
SEXUAL HARMONY
LUDWIG VAN BEETHOVEN, PROMETHEUS OF THE MODERN WORLD
BOOKS, OUR ETERNAL COMPANIONS
THE FIERY CHARIOTS
CREATIVE WORK: KARMA YOGA
THE ART OF STUDY: THE SORBONNE METHOD
COSMOS, MAN AND SOCIETY
I CAME BACK TOMORROW
THE BOOK OF LIVING FOODS
CREATIVE EXERCISES FOR HEALTH AND BEAUTY
SCIENTIFIC VEGETARIANISM
THE CONQUEST OF DEATH
HEALING WATERS
THE BOOK OF HERBS, VITAMINS, MINERALS

Book Design by Golondrina Graphics

CONTENTS

PREFACE

The Essene Gospel of Peace is one of the most extraordinary books in history. Since its first edition more than fifty years ago, it has been translated into seventeen languages and has had countless editions and reprints. In the United States alone and just during the last ten years it has been distributed in more than 215,000 copies. Yet none of its publishers—and there have been many, in various countries—have ever made financial profit from its tremendous popularity. They have, without exception, made the book available at cost, motivated by some unseen altruism to place the contents of the Essene Gospel within reach of everyone. And in all the many years since its first appearance, it has never been advertised commercially. Like the teachings of the first Christians, its message has always been carried from one seeker of truth to another.

After a hiatus of fifty years, volume two and three of the Essene Gospel of Peace were published in 1974, and already the first edition has been distributed to nearly every country of the world. New reprints are even now going to press. Just as their parents discovered volume one, so the sons and daughters of those religious revolutionaries of a generation past are discovering the ageless message of the Essene Gospel for the first time in these two books *(The Unknown Books of the Essenes* and *Lost Scrolls of the Essene Brotherhood*)* which at long last complete the task which began in the Secret Archives of the Vatican so many years ago.

*All three volumes of *The Essene Gospel of Peace,* as well as a complete catalogue of books by Edmond Bordeaux Szekely, are available from the International Biogenic Society, mailing address: *I.B.S. Internacional, Apartado 372, Cartago, Costa Rica, Central America.*

What is the miraculous magnet which attracts so many of the young spirits who are tired of the orthodox practices of the conventional churches? What makes the deserters of Christ rally to the living Essene Jesus? The answer may lie in something said to me this summer by a visitor to my forest retreat in British Columbia, where last year I finished the translation of volume two and three of the Essene Gospel.

His eyes shone as he told me, "No one can know my desolation when I left the Church. But my logical mind could no longer accept the empty rituals and fairy-tale beliefs. When I turned away from Christ, I embraced the philosophy of Nietzsche, and became a staunch atheist. But it was a hollow triumph, for my heart yearned to belong to something larger than myself, and reason alone could not fill the need to worship. Then I read the Essene Gospel of Peace. The truth shone from its pages with a golden light. I knew without being told that this was the real Christ, and what he taught was food for my soul as well as for my mind. Logic and love were combined in a beautiful union, and I felt that at last I had come home."

Looking at his face, so full of love and shining zeal, I could not help remembering lines from a favorite poem of my youth:

> *I had forgotten that my body is holy,*
> *because it is washed in the White River*
> *of Eternal Order:*
> *Miracle of miracles!*

I wish for this book no less a miracle but that the reader may also enter that Eternal White River and be baptized by the ancient truth of the Essene revelation.

EDMOND BORDEAUX SZEKELY

San Diego, California, 1975.

INTRODUCTION

Many words are devoted to St. Francis in this book, and with reason. In addition to all his other attributes, he was also the last personification of the Essene spirit. Since the gentle troubadour of God brought his message of love, purity and simplicity, no one has appeared who has represented so totally the Essene spirit.

With the coming of the industrial age, things of the spirit have assumed less and less reality in our lives, until now we have almost completely forgotten that we are born of the Earthly Mother and the Heavenly Father. The god of the twentieth century is technology—whose vast machines are wholly dependent on limited fuel sources—a computerized god we have programmed to produce material things, most of which we do not need and much of which is even harmful.

A good example of how our priorities have shifted in the last few hundred years is the reaction of the world to the discovery in 1945 of the Dead Sea Scrolls. True, there was great excitement. But it was the excitement of a major archeological find, not the celebration of a spiritual rebirth. The mass of books and articles that followed the discovery almost all dealt exclusively with dry technical details and confusing theological arguments, interspersed with commentaries on the commentaries, all punctuated with footnote after footnote.

What has happened to us? There was a time in our past when the very air crackled with wonder, when birds sang songs of mystery, and it was possible to meet a saint in bare feet on the dusty road, and soar with his spirit into unknown realms of holiness. Now euphoria is attained through drugs and self-destructive techniques, and religion, more often than not, is a matter of duty and righteousness, on the schedule every Sunday morning at eleven o'clock.

That state of wonder and awe before the miracle of life,

which burned so brilliantly in the Essene Brotherhood at the Dead Sea, and which faded out with the passing of the last Essene, St. Francis, was mine to kindle once more with the discovery of the Essene Gospel. It is a book of wonders, not only for the wisdom and guidance contained in its pages, but because it shines and glows with the lost spirit of ages past, when the distance between man and God was not so great, and when all of nature sang with the voice of angels.

The Essene Gospel is not the only manuscript of its kind in the Secret Archives of the Vatican. There were Gospels supposedly by Matthew, Barnabas, James, Peter and Thomas, used by the Manichaeans, together with the "Book of the Obstetrician," "The Essene Book of Genesis," "The Canto of Christ," "The Physiologist," written by "Essene heretics" and attributed to Ambrose, the pamphlets of Tertullian and the manuscripts of Simon the Magician. All these manuscripts were condemned as apocryphal and "damned for eternity" along with their authors and followers.

There was a time when the publication of any of these unknown writings would have stirred tremendous excitement among seekers of truth, and raging controversy among dedicated theologians. Now we are surprised at nothing. Nothing shocks us anymore. Ever since the first nuclear explosion, the realization of living on the brink of annihilation has altered irrevocably our perspective on life and death. Accustomed as we are to daily violence and terrorism in some part of the world, dispute over the authenticity of an apocryphal text seems unimportant and frivolous.

But fatalism and indifference will never solve the monumental problem of how to avert world catastrophe. We must involve ourselves again with the miracle of life. We have opened the Pandora's box of nuclear energy; we can also open with the key of truth the hidden treasure-house of ancient wisdom, waiting to be discovered in a forgotten manuscript, an ancient scroll, or in the unknown seat of knowledge within ourselves. We must rediscover our place in the world-picture, our original role as the partner of the Creator, helping to sow and harvest and make of the earth once more a Garden.

We must make our own discovery of the Essene Gospel. We must let St. Francis sing in our hearts.

They lived in the desert, on the shore of an ocean of sand. They came to this burning wasteland because it was less cruel than the persecution they suffered from their fellow man. And in the barren desert they planted a garden which grew and flourished for many hundreds of years. They guarded among them the most ancient knowledge and the greatest treasure of holiness the world had ever known. They were the Brotherhood of the Essenes.

Even they were not sure of their origins, so lost in time was the memory of their beginnings. Moses had been one of them, and the prophets of old. The Children of Light of ancient Sumeria were of their blood, and healers and teachers from the ancient time before the Pleistocene Cataclysm, which we call the Great Flood. The Brotherhood has always been with us.

When they had planted their garden in the desert, they watered it with loving care. They rose at dawn to commune with the Angels of the Earthly Mother, and to contemplate her manifold gifts. They praised the Angel of Sun in its rising and its setting, and they gathered the dew of morning from the desert plants, using it to bring the Angel of Water to the most arid of all places on the earth. They read from the Book of the Earthly Mother, and used their understanding to achieve total harmony with their environment. They communed with the Angels of the Heavenly Father at dusk, and learned from the Law how to bring the kiss of peace to the troubled brow of those who sought from them healing and help. They taught the Holy Law; they transcribed it with endless patience on scroll after scroll, that it might be perpetuated. They wrote songs of praise, of gladness, of sorrow. They shared the joys and griefs of men even as they overcame the limitations of humanity.

They sent out healers. And one of these was Jesus, the Essene. He walked among the sick and the troubled, and he brought them the knowledge they needed to cure themselves. Some who followed him wrote down what passed between him and those who suffered and were heavy-laden. The Elders of the Brotherhood made poetry of the words, and made unforgettable the story of the Healer of Men, the Good Shepherd. And when the time came at last for the Brothers to leave the desert and go to another place, the scrolls stayed behind as buried sentinels, as forgotten guardians of eternal and living truth.

A dark age began, a time of savagery, of barbarism, of book-burning, of superstition and worship of empty idols. The gentle Jesus was lost forever in the image of a crucified god, the Essene brothers hid their teachings in the minds of the few who could preserve them for their descendants, and the scrolls of healing lay neglected beneath the shifting shadows of the desert.

He was born in the middle of the fourth century at Stridon, in what is now Yugoslavia. His parents were well-to-do, and he was sent to Rome to continue his education when he was twelve. There he studied Latin literature and spent his free time exploring the catacombs, which held for him a mysterious attraction. Before he left Rome, he was baptized with the name of Jerome, by the same Church which would one day make him a Saint.

Jerome spent the next twenty years in travel, his restless mind searching for answers his formal education could not give him. Finally he turned, as so many seekers of truth had done before him, to the desert. He wandered through Chalcis for many years, adding the knowledge of Greek and Aramaic to his Latin, praying and learning to fast. He learned Hebrew from Jewish hermits, and from Rabbis who lived in the little towns scattered in the desert. He began to find fragments of ancient manuscripts in their possession, and with his new understanding of Hebrew started to decipher them. As he found more and more fragments, a mental picture began to form of a great truth of centuries past, a truth which reached far behind those centuries to the very beginning of history. He read in mysterious Hebrew letters of an ancient Brotherhood of the Desert, who lived according to the Law of laws, whose existence was in perfect harmony with heaven and earth, who enjoyed perfect health and lived much longer than ordinary men, who healed the sick, taught the ignorant, and radiated holiness to all who met them.

Not too far from his hidden valley, with date palms and a pristine spring, lived a retreat of anchorites, who Jerome was sure had descended from that mysterious Brotherhood of centuries past. They lived in little huts with irrigated gardens and small book cases in their window sills. They ate the fruits of the date palms and the herbs from their gardens, navigated through the desert by astral orientation, watching

the stars in the clear atmosphere of the desert, and woke at dawn and retired at dusk, each time communing with the Angels and contemplating the Heavenly Father. And they, too, had in their possession fragments of ancient manuscripts, containing the teachings upon which they based their lives. Jerome wrote to a friend: *Judei habent veritatem*—the Jews have the truth—and now Jerome possessed that truth, as well.

In the aftermath of a religious conflict, he left the desert and went to Antioch, there visiting the Nazarenes of Beroea to examine their copy of a Hebrew Gospel purporting to be original. His fame as a Hebrew scholar grew, and during this period he turned into Latin fourteen homilies on Jeremiah, fourteen on Ezekiel and nine on the sixth chapter of Isaiah. Again "the desert way" called to him, and he packed up his library and returned to his hermitage, accompanied by Innocent, Heliodorus, and a group of young followers. It was from this retreat that the summons from Rome came.

Pope Damasus, who later was canonized as St. Damasus, was a poet and archeologist, and the founder of the Papal Library. A lover of illuminations, he wrote his manuscripts in self-designed letters. But his most memorable service to our culture was his invitation to Jerome to leave his beloved desert and become his private secretary. For when the Pope recognized Jerome's profound knowledge of first century manuscripts, he not only made him papal secretary, but gave him the additional task of translating the New Testament.

The Latin translations of the second century, according to the Pope, through the constant copying and recopying by the scribes, had come to be "full of errors and dubious passages," so much so that each copy became a different version. Now Jerome unleashed his full creative power on a wealth of material, and while under the patronage of Pope Damasus, he not only completed the revision and completion of the Gospels, but also translated into Latin the Septuagint Psalter, the Song of Songs, the Proverbs and Ecclesiastes. He also translated the Book of Judith, the Book of Tobias and a number of "Apocryph Documents," among them the ancient Hebrew and Aramaic fragments of manuscripts which he had collected so long and so patiently. It was this last which provoked a storm of criticism and calumny.

Jerome himself wrote to Pope Damasus: "How far can I rectify the language of this version, carrying it back to the early days of its infancy? Is there a Christian, learned or unlearned, who will not accuse me with violent language and call me a forger and a profane person, for having the audacity to add anything to the old manuscripts or to make any changes or corrections therein?" His words were prophetic. While Pope Damasus lived, the veracity of Jerome's translations was not questioned. But with the death of his protector, and under the pressure of his great adversary, St. Augustine, the voices raised against him became an uproar, as when the denunciation of Jerome's translations by the Greek congregations forced the Bishops to ask the testimony of the Jewish residents. The majority of them sided with Jerome, but the constant turmoil was too much for a peaceful philosopher, and in August 385, Jerome left "Babylon" with a heavy heart and made his way to the Holy Land.

Again he pursued "the desert way to eternal life," and persisted in his search for Hebrew fragments, piecing together more and more of the story of the Essene Brotherhood. He continued his work in Bethlehem, producing in Latin a translation of the Old Testament, the Chronicles, the Book of Job, and Coptic ascetical works, among others. He directed the forming of a monastery, in which he tried to put into practice some of the Essene Way. Until his death, he never ceased his search for truth, his thirst for all-sided knowledge never sated.

After the death of St. Jerome, his manuscripts were scattered, including his Hebrew and Aramaic translations, but many of them reached sanctuary in the Secret Archives of the Vatican and eventually in the monastery of Monte Cassino. The stream was entering the river.

St. Benedict, the patron saint of all Europe, was born around the year 480 in Nursia, near what is now Spoleto, Umbria. He was sent by his provincial but cultured family to Rome, to be educated and begin his career. But the corruption of the decayed imperial city greatly shocked him, and he retired to the Subiaco area as a hermit. Later, he found a cave in the rocks beside a lake near the ruins of Nero's palace, and there he lived alone for three years. According to legend, he was fed by ravens, but more probably he was cared for by Romanus, a monk from one of the numerous monasteries nearby.

Somewhere in his search for truth, the young Benedict discovered St. Jerome's translations of the mysterious Hebrew fragments, just as Jerome had stumbled on the original, in his own search for truth many years before. The life of those first century Essenes must have been a glorious vision to the young hermit, tortured as he was by the threatening world chaos before him. A flowering branch of the eternal Tree of Life took root, grew and flourished in his mind. The Essene Brotherhood took shape as the Holy Rule of Benedict, that masterpiece of order and simplicity which gave rise to a monastic system that eventually saved Western culture from extinction during the Dark Ages. Alone in his cave, he felt himself a bridge between two worlds: the sun-filled radiance and order of the ancient brothers whose lives followed the harmony of nature and the cosmos, and the other barbaric and evil time that stretched before him like a chasm, threatening to engulf and drown all that man had so far created of wisdom and beauty. Benedict was determined this should not happen, and summoned the Essene Brothers out of the past to help him.

Disciples began to flock to him. He left his cave and founded twelve monasteries, each with twelve monks. His fame grew, and with it the inevitable attempts to destroy him.

St. Benedict
Detail from Fresco by Fr. Dunstan Massey, Westminster Abbey, Mission, B.C., Canada

As he had turned away from Rome, so he departed from the intrigues, and with a few disciples turned his eyes to the summit of a hill rising steeply above Cassino, halfway between Rome and Naples.

Monte Cassino was destined to become a beautiful, organized fortress of security and order amid the surrounding chaos of invasion, disorientation and confusion. It would become one of two magnetic poles of western civilization, the other being the Vatican. Just as the Essenes guarded the Holy Law during the troubled era of the first century, so did the Benedictine monks guard and copy in their Scriptoria, which played the role of medieval publishing houses, the works of Cicero, Seneca, Tacitus, St. Jerome and St. Augustine, Philo of Alexandria, Josephus Flavius, and many more, all of which would have been trampled to shreds under the heel of the warriors who would soon tear Europe apart.

From the highest point of Monte Cassino, one could see the whole length of the green valley of Iri. The monastery itself consisted of a fortress, a pagan temple and a sacred grove. Monte Cassino and the other Benedictine monasteries were economically self-sufficient, self-contained, secluded cities, well able to resist the turbulence of the world. Within its enclave were all the preconditions of life: springs, vegetable gardens, orchards, fields of growing grain, oven for baking (the monks baked their own bread as well as continuously copying their books), materials for the artist and the artisan, as well as a library of a great number of books and manuscripts studied and read in the Scriptorium.

But of all the Essene echoes which resounded in the world of Benedict, perhaps the most beautiful and long-lasting was his *Regula Santa,* or the Holy Rule. This was a highly logical and practical Code of Ethics for the communal living of the monks, working to their greatest benefit and usefulness. In practically every way, the Rule interpreted and adapted to medieval times the way of life of the Essene Brotherhoods. All things were owned in common. The Abbot, elected for life by the monks, had supreme power but was obliged to seek the counsel of the elders, his final decision on any matter being between himself and God. Thus he represented both Man and the Creator, working together as partners in the never-ending task of Creation. He appointed his own officials—prior, novice-master, guestmaster, and the rest—but although every detail of their behavior is outlined and laid down with precision, a strong current of humanity, of brotherly love, flows through the Rule, in this aspect unique among all the monastic and religious rules of the Middle Ages, and proving the link to the Essene traditions. The wise balance of prayer, work and study—*ora et labora*—the care given to the body, with time divided wisely between rest, exercise and proper food, the importance given to gardening and cultivation of the fields, the love of music and art, and above all, the courtesy given to each and every guest, as if he were the Lord himself, all these were much closer to life in the Brotherhoods at the Dead Sea, than they were to medieval Europe. The character of Benedict shines through all the words of his Rule: wisdom tempered with love; order and authority tempered with compassion.

A copy of the Regula Santa sent to Rome was lost, but a handwritten copy by the Saint himself remained in Monte Cassino. During the Lombard invasion the monks fled to Rome with this original copy, a pound weight for bread and a measurement for fruits (the monks were permitted daily one pound of bread, one pint of milk and one quart of fruit). All these relics were returned to Monte Cassino in the middle of the eighth century by Pope Zachary. In the ninth century, many manuscripts were destroyed by the marauding Saracens. A remaining fragment of the Regula Santa survived until the Napoleonic wars when the last original parchment written by St. Benedict was lost.

A few important fragments nevertheless survived, giving evidence of the original Essene traditions as written down by St. Jerome, that indefatigable translator of so many first century texts.

The original Essene "Peace be with you," became "Seek peace and pursue it." (Prologue)

The Essene Gospel's supreme law, "Love your brothers, for your Heavenly Father is love, for your Earthly Mother is love, for the Son of Man is love," was clothed in a Benedictine garment: "In the first place to love the Lord God with our whole heart, our whole soul, our whole strength, then our neighbor as ourselves." (Chapter 4)

The Essene teaching on the Heavenly Father and his Angels, and their praise and guidance to live in harmony with them, "and so shall his Angels know that you walk in His paths," took this admonition: "Let us therefore think well how we ought to behave under the eyes of God and his angels, and so stand to sing the psalms that our mind may be in harmony with our voice." (Chapter 19)

The communal life and works performed in the Essene Brotherhoods, so beautifully described by Josephus, Philo and Plinius, strongly survives in Chapter 48 of St. Benedict's Holy Rule: "Then are they truly monks when they live by the labor of their hands, as did our fathers and the Apostles."

Divine love was the universal guidance for the Essene elders, the heads of each community, and that same divine love flows through Benedict's advice to the Abbot in Chapter 64: "Let him so temper all things that the strong may have something to strive after, and the weak nothing at which to take alarm."

The basic teaching of the Essene Gospel: "And so love your true brothers as your Heavenly Father and Earthly Mother love them," becomes Chapter 72 of the Holy Rule: "Let them cherish mutual love chastely as brothers. Let them fear God lovingly. Let them love their Abbot with sincere and humble charity. Let them put absolutely nothing before Jesus, and may he bring us all together to Life Eternal."

St. Benedict wrote in his Holy Rule that there would always be guests at his monastery, and made it a law in Chapter 53: "All visitors who call are to be welcomed as if they were Jesus himself." The more than a thousand years that have passed since he created his monastery at Monte Cassino have proven his words to be true. Visitors always find an atmosphere of the Sevenfold Peace, an invitation to communion with the Angels in a constant divine presence of a living community, offering a daily round of communions.

Miraculously, the monasteries of St. Benedict have, for the most part, remained relatively unscathed by the many wars fought outside the peaceful walls. Even in 1943, the German officials were kind enough to warn the Abbot of Monte Cassino that within a few days the monastery would be the center of decisive and fierce battles with awesome artillery duels. Under the direction of the Abbot, hundreds of monks improvised wooden crates and packed together the priceless contents of the rare manuscripts, scrolls and codices, representing Greek and Roman classics, the most important works of the patristics and scholastics, and more than forty thousand invaluable parchments.

All these found safety and shelter in the Secret Archives of the Vatican.

THE OCEAN

One of the most unique, exceptional human beings in history was St. Francis. He is one of the very few Catholic saints who cannot be confined within the limits of one religion or philosophy: he belongs to the world.

Like the young Prince Gautama Buddha, who left his father's kingdom to search for the truth in the forests of ancient India, Francis also understood at an early age the futility and hopelessness of the materialistic world, based on greed and egoism. They both realized that in the ocean of suffering of mankind, the most important thing is to remedy that suffering immediately. There is both ageless wisdom and modern effectiveness in this approach. If your house is on fire, said Buddha, the first thing to do is get out of the house. Thus did the young Francis leave his father's treasure-house, naked and without possessions, to dedicate himself to simplicity, the treasure of the poor, and to offer an unforgettable spiritual banquet to all who met him traveling the roads of Italy.

The young Buddha and the young Francis. . . they were two streaks of lightning in the dark sky of mankind, which they found hopelessly enmeshed in a tangle of ignorance, violence and thirst for self-exploiting pleasures. With untold compassion they looked on the sons of men always filled with insatiable desires of the flesh, always losing health and peace of mind in a quagmire of ephemeral possessions.

And as the lightning flash reveals the earth in blinding clarity, so did their lives of pristine simplicity and purity betray in harsh relief the misery and ignorance surrounding them. They both established the true kingdom of the spirit in their hearts, and successfully united all the forces of life against the forces of death.

It is not surprising that today's youth has discovered both spiritual giants as kindred spirits, whom they can uncon-

ditionally trust. They see a revolutionary spirit like their own, and disillusionment with the sterile, stereotyped aimlessness of the pompous establishment, based on rigid authority and the worship of the golden calf. They both represent to the youth of today the hope and return to the eternal spirituality of the soul, and simplicity of nature, both forming the last chance of escape from the widening chasm of mankind's self-destruction.

St. Francis was the ocean to the river of St. Benedict, the stream of St. Jerome, the hidden source of the Essene Brotherhood. He is important to this story because of what he was, not for what he discovered. Francis did not have to look for sacred scrolls; the word of God was engraved in his heart. He was a spiritual reincarnation of those who wrote the scrolls, a twelfth-century composite of all the Essene brothers who ever lived. He sang to his beloved birds about the angels of sun, water, joy and peace. He would not wear shoes, so as to always feel the Earthly Mother beneath his feet. He slept at night in the open, wherever he might be when night fell, for the precious stars of his Heavenly Father would shine over his head no matter where he laid it down. His rule was simply "to follow the teachings of Jesus and to walk in his footsteps." And no one in history has ever done so with such joyous perseverance. Through the towns and villages of Italy he wandered, as his Essene brothers a thousand years earlier had done in Galilea, healing the sick, teaching the ignorant, and sharing his message of love and compassion with all who would listen.

Several times he stayed with the Benedictine monks of Monte Cassino, where the pure and simple life, lived in poverty, chastity and obedience, was the inspiration for his own Regula for his friars. And when he and his hermits awoke at dawn, they raised their arms toward the sun, rain and wind with the same fervor as did their Essene brothers around the Dead Sea so many centuries before. The Canticle to the Sun and the Essene Gospel are essentially identical, the reverence for life, inherent in the Essene spirit, traveling intact over the centuries.

He had no erudition, no book knowledge, and no authority. But he drew from the Eternal Sea of Wisdom and Love abundant spiritual power to renew the stagnant church. He had the key to open eternity.

And open it he did, with his arms outstretched to all of God's creatures, all his brothers and sisters. To him, all nature was a mirror of God, and man the most blessed of all, with the strength of the earth in his limbs and the light of the Heavenly Father on his brow. And with absolute faith and joyous courage, St. Francis created an oasis of light in the bleak Dead Sea of the middle ages.

He was not only a reborn Essene—he was the very fulfillment of the Essene Gospel of Peace.

MY LATIN AND GREEK EDUCATION
IN THE PIARIST ORDER

Cognoscere est cognoscere causas. To know is to know the origin, said the Roman philosopher, Lucretius. So, I will start at the very beginning.

It all started with a kind of Potsdam agreement between my father, a Transylvanian Unitarian, and my mother, a French Catholic. One may only wonder at the strength of the loving bond which held them together, as their religious beliefs were light-years apart. One of my father's ancestors was the co-founder of Unitarianism in Transylvania, a close friend of Francis David, who wrote his revolutionary book, "The Unity of God," while my father's ancestor wrote the first "Universal History" in central Europe, both using the same printing press brought with them from Germany, one during the day, the other during the night hours. In contrast, one of my mother's ancestors was a Cardinal of France and the author of a voluminous medieval work on "The Divine Authority of the Church." My father followed the Unitarian principles that we shall never accept anything which contradicts common sense, and every member of the congregation should be free to form whatever ideas he may have about God, Life and the Universe. My mother devoutly believed in the mystery of the Holy Trinity of the Father, Son and Holy Ghost.

Such was the background of differing parental philosophies when the subject of my education became a matter of decision. And in a spirit of conciliation, they reached the following agreement: first, I would be educated in a Catholic monastery of the Piarist order, which specialized in classical education, with the emphasis on Greek, Latin and Ecclesiastic literature. Then, after graduating from the Piarist school, I would go to the University of Paris, completing my education at the Sorbonne for my doctorate in philosophy. After that, it would be up to me to decide what profession and what religion I would choose for myself.

And so I began my scholastic life with the Piarist order. At first, it was very difficult to get used to the austerity of Piarist life after the luxuries of our affluent home (my father owned large estates both in Transylvania and in France): to wake up at dawn to go to Mass, to wash with cold water in unheated rooms, to personify all the long hours of the day the famous watchword of the Piarist order: *Ora et Labora*— pray and study. If we wanted a piece of bread, or even a glass of water, we had to ask for it in perfect Latin. But in retrospect, I am eternally grateful for my training in discipline and will power and my resultant proficiency in classic Greek and Latin philology and literature.

When I was eighteen years old, I was speaking classic Greek and Latin fluently and graduated *magna cum laude,* becoming the valedictorian of my class. At the same time, I prepared my obligatory thesis for graduation, with the title, "Let St. Francis Sing in your Heart." It was a labor of love, and I wrote it effortlessly, never imagining the chain of events it would set into motion.

Right after my graduation, I was called to the office of our Headmaster, Msgr. Mondik, the Prior of the monastery. When I entered, he looked up from my thesis which he had been glancing through, and smiled.

"Well, my son," he said, "you are now ready to fly out to the great and harsh world. Some time soon, Satan will show you all the temptations of a life full of pleasure and luxury. So I have decided to beat Satan and steer you instead toward a great spiritual experience. I have here a letter of introduction for you to my old schoolmate, the Prefect of the Archives of the Vatican. With this letter, the doors of the Archives will be open to you, so you may find out everything about our beloved St. Francis, as you expressed your wish to do so in your thesis." Seeing the sudden enthusiasm on my face, he raised his hand and continued in a more serious tone: "But, my son, there is a price to pay for this privilege. During your studies under the Prefect of the Vatican, you must subject yourself to the vow of Poverty, Chastity and Obedience of the Franciscan monks, and live accordingly. You must dress and live in the simplest possible way, and eat only black bread, cheese, fruit and vegetables. And nothing else. I know your family has great wealth, but during this time you shall not accept one penny from them." He held up an envelope. "Here you will find a very modest sum in Italian currency, corresponding to the salary of the poorest unskilled worker in Italy. And you must live like one. But, on the other hand, you will enjoy a spiritual banquet to be able to study under my friend, Msgr. Mercati, and have at your disposal the inexhaustible treasures of the ages in the Archives and Library of the Vatican. Well, my son, are you willing to make the great sacrifice?"

I was stupefied, unable to speak. Awed by the prospect of this tremendous opportunity, I could not find words to express my gratitude. Fortunately, our beloved headmaster was as sensitive and understanding as he was wise and learned. He smiled and nodded, as if to say he knew what was going on in my mind, and handed me the envelope and the letter of introduction, saying, "I will mail to my friend separately your thesis on St. Francis. It is a very promising one and I am sure he will enjoy it. Go with God, my son."

He gave me his blessing and I found myself wandering through the monastery grounds in a daze, conscious only of the precious letter in my hand.

(Before going on, I would like to quote here an excerpt from that thesis on St. Francis which opened the heart of my Piarist headmaster, and as a result, the doors of the Archives of the Vatican. Please forgive the spiritual flamboyance; I was only eighteen.)

ST. FRANCIS

We see the face of Saint Francis and his smile, like a glimpse of our first love, or of our lost Eden. This smile of gratitude and humility is the mystery of one of the strongest, strangest and most original figures in human history. His eyes! They glowed with the fire which consumed him, night and day. He loved nature as a parent loves his children, each one a unique and cherished individual. When he walked in a forest, he did not see the forest as a whole, but each tree alone—he wanted to see each tree as a separate, almost sacred thing, a child of God and therefore a brother or sister of man. He was a poet, and his whole life was a poem. His brotherhood with the sun and moon, with the water and fire, is so beautifully expressed in his Canticle to Brother Sun. He sang it while wandering in the meadows, pouring skyward all the passions of a poet. This hymn, so full of the mirth of youth and the memories of childhood, runs through his whole life like a refrain.

THE CANTICLE TO THE SUN

Praise be to Thee, O Lord,
For all Thy creatures,
And especially for our Brother, the Sun,
Who gives us the day,
And who shows forth Thy light,
Fair is he and radiant with great splendor:
To us he is the symbol of Thee, O Lord.

Praise be to Thee, O Lord,
For our sister, the moon,
And for the stars.
Thou hast set them clear,
Beautiful and precious

In the heavens above.

Praise be to Thee, O Lord,
For our brother, the wind,
For the air and the clouds,
For the clear sky and for all weathers,
By which Thou givest life
And the means of life
To all Thy creatures.

Praise be to Thee, O Lord,
for our brother, fire,
By whom Thou givest us
Light in the darkness.
He is beautiful and bright,
Courageous and strong.

Praise be to Thee, O Lord,
For our sister, water,
Who is so useful to us,
Humble, precious and chaste.

Praise be to Thee, O Lord,
For our mother, the earth,
Who sustains and nourishes us,
Bringing forth diverse fruits,
Flowers of many colors,
And the grass.

THE BROTHERS

The other day I looked down on the lake. And I saw our whole town upside down. We thought to make our town safer and more permanent with massive foundations and watchtowers and the high citadel overlooking everything. But the moment one sees it upside down, the very same strength and might is what is the most vulnerable! The whole world seemed to hang on a thin, God-given thread—I suddenly saw everything in a new light of eternal danger and utter dependence on divine grace. And I fervently gave thanks from the bottom of my heart to God Almighty that the world had not been chopped and shattered into falling stars!

The less a man thinks of himself, the more he thinks of his good luck and of all the miraculous gifts of God. For there is no way a man can earn a star, or deserve a sunset. We should be infinitely grateful to the Creator for all the immensely beautiful gifts we receive from Him every day of our lives. Ever since we were born, when we received the first gift, the gift of Life, we have been endlessly showered with gifts from God: the starry sky, the mountains with their peaks lost in the clouds, the forests full of God's creatures, the ocean with its vast power, music, books, travel, friendship, love. I am so overwhelmed by His generosity that I am trying to pay back all that I can. I have such a debt to my Creator that I will never be able to pay back even a fraction of what He has given me. But He never asks me to pay back anything; and this is why I am trying to pay back at least something every day. But I am selfish, for I know that the more I try to pay back, the more He will give me. I try to show Him how grateful I am for all of His wonderful gifts, just to receive more and more from Him. When we have seen the whole world hanging by a hair at the mercy of God, then we have seen the truth. From that moment, all our thoughts, all our feelings are transformed into pure joyful thanks for the infinite love of God. When we know that we can never repay our boundless debt, we gladly dedicate ourselves to a lifetime of trying to repay it, in an ecstasy of joy and thanksgiving. This is why we who are ragged, penniless and homeless, yet come forth shouting and singing such songs as might come from the stars! Because the stars, passing above us in their radiance, look down on us, the children of God, with envy!

35

MY UNFORGETTABLE FIRST DAY IN ROME

It was with mixed feelings that I left the spiritual island where I had spent the last eight years of my life, and entered the unknown ways of the world outside. My parents whole-heartedly approved of my plans. "A wonderful adventure," said my Unitarian father, with a twinkle in his eye. "A great spiritual pilgrimage," said my Catholic mother, with reverence in her voice.

At my father's suggestion, I went first to Paris and Leipzig, to visit the special bookstores he had indicated, in order to obtain the best Aramaic and Hebrew dictionaries. He had told me, "I don't worry about your Greek and Latin, but without a working knowledge of Aramaic and Hebrew, you will be lost, my son."

About ten days later, I found myself on an Italian train, in simple attire, the dictionaries in one of my two suitcases, my letter of introduction and the envelope with its meager portion of Italian lira in my pocket. I looked through the window of the train at the scenes of the Italian countryside coming and going from view: peasants working in the fields, women washing laundry in the creeks, and playing children gaily greeting us from the distance. It was a Saturday, and groups of noisy young men boarded our wagon, going to their soccer game in the next town. There were elderly men and women on their way to visit their children, and whole families going to visit relatives. Italian exuberance filled our wagon, and I had plenty of opportunity to practice my rudimentary Italian during the long trip.

Finally, in the evening, we arrived to "The City." My first experiences were not very auspicious. The railroad sta-tion, crowded with jostling people, full of the smoke of the locomotives, and heavy with the smell of cheap wine and greasy food, dampened greatly my enthusiasm for "The Holy City." After some searching, I found a fiacre, with a sleepy coachman and a sad-looking horse. With the best use of my rather limited Italian vocabulary, I tried to explain to him that I was a student and I needed an inexpensive room for the night. "Ah, a student," he said, sleepily, as if that explained everything, and urged his even sleepier horse into motion. After a fairly long journey through strange-looking, narrow streets full of people sitting before their gates, standing in groups, loafing and watching the passers-by, we finally arrived to a small, two-story house with an open gate leading to a tiny, dark lobby where an old man, reeking of wine and tobacco, received us. I gave the coachman half a lira, which he good-naturedly put in his pocket, complaining with a murmur, "Students!" as he drove away. And so I was left with my two suitcases, one full of dictionaries, the other just as full of almonds. "Come, student," said the old man, leading me to what must have been his worst room. "One lira," he said, extending his palm. "If you stay longer, it will be five lira a week. Buona notte!" And he shuffled away.

The room had no light, but the street light from the nearest lamp post rather mistily indicated the existence of an old bed with a straw mattress, and an old chair and table with very shaky legs. After trying unsuccessfully to lock the door, I put my two suitcases under the bed, undressed, and vowed to put all unpleasantness out of my mind and have a good sleep. But as soon as I began to drift off, I heard a dreaded droning sound as dozens of mosquitoes began darting attacks on my face and arms. Trying to fend them off, I realized with horror that they were not my only company: large cockroaches were walking up and down my body as if they owned the bed, which they probably did. In spite of the stifling heat of the room, my only defense was to dress up again and lie down with a handkerchief over my face. But still a night's sleep was not to be mine. Just as I thought I had discouraged the mosquitoes and cockroaches, a tremendous noise from the lobby jolted me wide awake. An extremely boisterous party had started, with one basso profundo singing some operatic arias and everyone else joining in, clinking glasses, laughing, shouting, and so forth. As I lay, engulfed by the noise, I realized to my great sorrow that this was Saturday night, and the party would probably go on for hours. And so it did. Every time the basso voice stopped, there were gleeful shouts of "more, Giorgio, more!" and, sadly, Giorgio continued, trying to make up with deafening volume what he lacked in musical quality. The off-key singing and the shouts of "Bravo!" and "more, Giorgio!" continued, interminably it seemed, until finally the merrymakers went home by the full light of morning, and I was at last able to sleep for an hour or two.

When I awoke, I realized without a doubt that the sooner I found a quiet room somewhere, the better. I politely returned the bed to the cockroaches and looked for some water, but in spite of the existence of a cracked lavoir, there was not a drop in the room. So I picked up my two suitcases and made my way to the lobby, which did not look much better by daylight. But there was a nice young clerk, who kindly answered my questions, and when I asked him if he could tell me where I could find a quiet room, he took me to a table on the other side of the lobby, where two men were playing chess, their game watched with great excitement by half a dozen spectators. The young clerk told me I should wait for the end of the game, because the two chess players were living in a very quiet pensione and perhaps they could help me to find it. I discovered later that the two players, one employed by the railroad, the other by a bank, were the chessmasters of the neighborhood, and a game of theirs was always an "event." Although I did not say a word, I could not help registering the different moves with my facial expressions, and they soon became aware of me, even favoring me with a smile now and then. They knew I was a chess player, and a good one, just by the expressions involuntarily moving over my face. Soon it became apparent that one of the players was becoming very uncomfortable, as his position on the chessboard started to crumble. Finally, he asked per-

mission to go to the men's room, and motioned for me to
take his place until his return. I did so gladly, and he must
have been very constipated, because it was at least half an
hour before he returned. Meanwhile, I tried to salvage his
position from the defeat which was inevitable. After several
moves, although I was unable to gain any decisive advantage,
I at least achieved a draw, at which point my friend returned.
"Bravo, bravissimo!" he shouted happily, when he saw he
had been saved from defeat, and invited me to join them for
lunch and then to a tremendous soccer game between Rome
and Milano. When I explained to them in my halting Italian
that I was a poor student looking for a simple, inexpensive
and quiet room, they both exclaimed simultaneously, "La
Signora!" A torrent of excited talk followed, and I finally
understood that they would be happy to take me to their
pensione, but only after the soccer game and they would not
hear of my refusing to accompany them!

So, after lunch, I found myself on a lurching fiacre with
the two chessplayers, on our way to the soccer game, which
we finally reached after a long ride. I was uncomfortable
about leaving my suitcases, but they assured me that the
coachman was a relative of theirs and a very honest man who
would wait for us with his fiacre until the game was over,
when he would take us all to the Signora. And that is how
my first day in Rome was spent at a soccer game, still a
long way from my much-desired quiet room! But it was an
exciting game, and the time passed quickly. Finally we were
back in the slow-moving fiacre, discussing all the details of
the game, and my mood became more and more mellow, as
we got closer to my promised land, the quiet room.

We at last drew up before a friendly little house on a
small side street (it was quiet!). They took me immediately
to the by-now famous Signora, who turned out to be a rather
voluminous lady with great authority and kind eyes. My first
question to her was to inquire how far away the Vatican
was, and she assured me I could walk there in an hour. This

seemed reasonable, but then we encountered an unexpected obstacle: it appeared, in spite of the warm recommendations of my new friends, who by now had taken me completely under their protection, that the Signora did not have a room to rent! The only vacant room in the pensione would be occupied in two days. The chessplayers argued, the Signora argued, I listened quietly, and finally a stalemate developed. The Signora agreed to rent to me the single vacant room at the end of the corridor, but only for two days. I was only too glad to accept the proposition, as by this time I was really ready for a good sleep.

At long last, the promised land was mine, and within the hour I was sleeping in a comfortable bed in a simple, but clean and *quiet* little room.

When I arose the next morning, my two chessplaying friends and practically all the other inhabitants of the house had left for work, and I found only the voluminous Signora seated at a white-covered table in the corridor, having her breakfast. On the wall behind her, and dominating the room, was a huge portrait of her late lamented husband, a shining example of bourgeois elegance. His cravat was starched and spotless, his hair, brilliant with pomade, was parted with painful symmetry, and his fierce eyebrows competed with a pair of magnificent moustaches. His commanding presence, however, was limited to the gilt-edged frame around his portrait; it was very clear that the Signora was now the sole authority of the household.

She invited me to join her, and I accepted. She told me that the two chessplayers had been living in her pensione for several years, and that they had recommended me highly to her, feeling confident she would be able to solve the room-finding problems of a poor student with very little money. Then, after explaining again that my present room was already spoken for, she said that the only possible solution she could see for my problem was to live on the roof! My surprised expression must have shown that I thought she was teasing me, so she got up from the table and motioned for me to follow. I did, and she led me to a small staircase which we climbed up to the roof, which turned out to be a large, spacious area commanding a wonderful view of the city. She led me to a tiny storage room at one end, chock-full of old junk which she said had belonged to her grandfather, and which was very precious to her. She told me that a night watchman had been living in it, but he got married a few days ago and left. She said if I would be willing to sleep there every night, she would be equally willing to let me live there free. I noticed there were some pieces of lumber in the little room, and I asked her if she would be willing to let me have them, plus a handful of nails and the loan of a hammer, and I could improvise a roof, saying that I would rather sleep under it than in the dirty storage room. She gladly consented, and in two days I had an acceptable roof above my head, an old bed from the storage to sleep on, one large wooden box for a table and bookshelf, and one small box to sit on. My two chessplaying friends climbed to the roof to inspect my improvised installation, and they both expressed approval of my spontaneous carpentry, adding that the Signora had made a good bargain, as the night watchman had charged her five lira a week. I assured them that I was very grateful to them for bringing me here, as well as to the Signora for letting me stay. After inviting me to play chess with them every Sunday, they left, but returned later with a gift: an empty five-gallon can, to bring and keep my water in, telling me triumphantly that they had persuaded the Signora to let me use the wash-room below. It was only the beginning of a strong and proven friendship which lasted throughout my stay, and I will always remember their gentle faces and ritual chess games.

In the afternoon of the second day, I ventured out to explore the neighborhood. My little pensione was surrounded by a cobweb of narrow, cobblestone streets, lined with small houses and peopled by simple, good-natured folk. I found a great number of small stores, with dozens of simple things to sell, such as kerosene for the lamps, sugar, flour, fat, oil, cereals (all these in open barrels), a few fruits, vegetables, and all kinds of candy, the displays of which were always surrounded by children asking plaintively what they could buy for a penny. I was satisfied I would not starve, and on the third day, I took my letter of introduction and started off for the Vatican.

It took some time to orient myself amid the labyrinth of those little streets, but within a few days I found my way easily and never got lost again. The narrow streets and little stores, the gentle, smiling people greeting me as I made my daily trek to the Vatican, the happy children with their small pieces of candy, all come back to my mind even after half a century, part of the tapestry of those first days when I became part of this typical Italian neighborhood, a friendly little city-within-a-city.

My adventure began in June of 1923. Two years later, in the fall of 1925, I stood before my classmates at the University of Paris and read aloud my thesis, as it was tradition at the Sorbonne for each student to write a lecture once a year and read it to his class. The subject of my thesis was the extraordinary story of my studies in the Archives of the Vatican, and it was extremely well received by both my classmates and my professor. Though the manuscript of the thesis was lost many years ago, the story remains indelibly etched in my memory, and I would like now to share it with my readers,

45

I remember well the first time I followed the arched road leading past the Osservatore Romano building to the court of the Belvedere, the seat of the Secret Archives, next to the Vatican Library.

When I entered the labyrinths of the Archives, I forgot completely the life of the city outside, for it was truly a world in itself. I felt very young and lost as I contemplated the endless corridors, vaulted archways and mysterious doors, all leading to more endless corridors. And everywhere, lining the shelves which reached dimly beyond my vision, were countless stacks of scrolls, codices, ancient manuscripts and disjointed papers.

Miraculously, I somehow found my way to the outer office of Monsignor Angelo Mercati, the Prefect of the Archives, and the boyhood friend of my Headmaster, Msgr. Mondik. It was to him that my letter of introduction was addressed, and I held it like a talisman as I passed yet another awesome-looking Swiss Guard, standing in immobile splendor at the door. My letter must have satisfied them, because they allowed me to pass. (Yet they never failed to ask me for my pass before letting me descend the stairway to the Archives, even though I soon became well-known.) In the outer office, the Secretary was kind and patient with me, but made it very clear that not just anyone might interrupt Msgr. Mercati, but if I would leave my letter with him he would give it to the Prefect at the proper time and I should return tomorrow at the same hour. This was indeed a blow—greater even than my disappointment at not meeting Msgr. Mercati was my reluctance to give up my precious letter. But I was resolved to be faithful to my pledge of obedience, so I gave him the letter and left, finding the teeming and noisy city a shocking contrast to the solemn peace within those ancient walls.

How that day passed I do not remember. I only recall

that I had to use great self-control to overcome my anxiety. Would I then not be accepted as a student after all? Had I offended in some way unknown to me? These anxious thoughts were calmed as I again entered the majesty and peace of Vatican City. This time I found my way to the office of Msgr. Mercati with greater ease, and this time I was allowed to enter an inner room. I found myself in a warm, friendly, book-lined study, with a huge and ancient desk behind which sat one of the most unforgettable figures who would ever enter my life.

This was the renowned Msgr. Angelo Mercati, Prefect of the Vatican Archives, and author of more than a dozen books on philosophical and theological subjects, being a noted authority in patristic and scholastic literature and in subjects pertaining to first and second century Church history. The titles of some of his works indicate his multilateral interests: "Peter, the Sinner," "The Private Libraries of the Popes," "Ancient Art," "Monte Cassino," "Michelangelo," "Copernicus," etc. I was also to discover later that he had an incredible, almost superhuman memory, embracing the entire 25-mile length of the long shelves of the Archives.

But at the moment, all I could see and understand was the penetrating warmth of his eyes, a look of such utter benevolence mingled with profound wisdom, that I was rendered speechless as he motioned for me to be seated.

"I have read your thesis, my son," he said. "Can you tell me why you are here, and what you are looking for?"

I told him, as simply as I could, about my love for St. Francis, and that I wanted to know what he had known, to discover the source of that most original and unique of thinkers. In short, I opened my heart to him, revealing much I had never told another.

He was silent for a long time. Then he said, very quietly, "St. Francis is the Ocean. You must find the River nourishing it, just as he did. And then you must look for the Stream.

And then, if your feet are firmly on the Path, you will seek out the Source."

I wanted to ask him the meaning of his words, but his look stopped me. "Go with God, my son," he murmured, and it was both a benediction and a dismissal.

Now that I was accepted as a student, the world of the Archives became my world, and even during the long walk back to my roof-top at the Signora's, I still saw in my mind's eye the dozens of subdivisions in those endless halls and corridors, the Archivum Arcis, the Miscelanea, the Instrumenta, the Miscelanea Fondi and the index room, where the students struggled to make sense out of the over six hundred handwritten indexes, which were woefully incomplete.

But the attendants and staff of the archives were kind and helpful, and gave to the students general guidance, mainly in the index room. After that, it was up to the students to carry on their individual researches. And I felt somewhat like a small boy standing on an immense seashore, trying to pick up a few pebbles. At first, I did not know where to begin, for while the Vatican Library is mainly a large collection of individual books, the Secret Archives of the Vatican comprise more than 25 miles of bookshelves of scrolls, parchments, paper manuscripts and codices. Much of the Secret Archives is still terra incognita. In one square, dust-filled room there were over ten thousand packages of unexamined documents!

My fellow students represented almost every country in the world, and we shared a fraternal atmosphere of love, devotion and dedication. Some were students like myself, some were foreign priests, others were officials on unknown missions, but we all ate together our noon meal in a spirit of brotherhood in a courtyard patio, surrounded by trees, flowers and the fragrance of hundreds of orange blossoms. And while my fellow students shared with me their meager portions of cheese, bread and fruits, we would tell each other our spiritual experiences while searching in our microcosmos.

For some time, I immersed myself in Latin and Greek documents, using my fluency in those languages to delve into everything known about St. Francis. During the late morning hours, always amidst great excitement among the students, Msgr. Mercati made his regular tour of the study room, answering attentively whatever question was asked of him. He had been watching my efforts for some time, and one day, during his rounds, he told me, "Remember, my son, the Latin Ocean is nourished by the Greek River, which is nourished by the Aramaic Stream, which originates from the Hebrew Source." And he assigned to me an Aramaic-Hebrew guide, a French monk with whom I became fast friends.

My work progressed. My search began to take shape, and the enigmatic words of my spiritual mentor began to take on meaning. I also started to notice with new interest a large, permanently closed door near the end of the lower corridor leading from Msgr. Mercati's office, to which only the Prefect had the key. I also gathered courage to descend a mysterious, circular staircase which led to the oldest part of the Secret Archives, where the most precious and most ancient documents were kept. It was also at this time that I started my investigations of the fifteen enormous closets of the Miscelanea. Suddenly I knew I was on the track, and I also knew what my next step must be.

When I approached Msgr. Mercati to ask his permission to visit the archives of the Benedictine monastery of Monte Cassino, there was an unmistakable twinkle in his eye as he handed me from his desk a letter of recommendation to the Abbot, dated the day before. He enjoyed my astonishment. "Go with God, my son. I think you have found the River."

I spent many weeks at this most ancient of western monasteries, which in its long life had suffered everything from Saracen invasions to fire and earthquake (and twenty years later would be in the path of the heavy artillery of the German army), and each time its destruction was followed by a glorious rebirth, stronger and more beautiful than before.

I felt the awesome magnitude of the task that Benedict had set before his monks: to collect, to copy and to preserve all the best of literature, art and music that man had created, so that when the dark ages would be over, he could once again find his past and his origins.

That was not all I felt and learned at Monte Cassino. When I saw the monks walking in the grove and working in the garden, eating their bread and fruits together at their communal meal, meditating in their small, individual cells, singing together of the glory of God at morning and evening, I could not help remembering Josephus' beautiful description of life in the Essene brotherhoods at the Dead Sea. And in the archives of Monte Cassino, I made the acquaintance of the gentle St. Benedict, who transformed an ancient dream into a reality which became a bulwark for the western world.

I returned to Msgr. Mercati. He looked at me silently with those penetrating eyes. "Did you find the Stream also, my son?"

"Not yet, Father," I replied, "but I shall!"

He fixed me with another probing look, then slowly nodded his head, and after a long pause said, "Yes, you will." And he handed me a key which I knew was to the locked room at the end of the corridor.

"Be sure to return this to my own hands," he told me. "And good luck, my son!"

I entered the secret room as an initiate of old must have entered the sacred chamber of the Great Pyramid, and this time I did not take my Aramaic guide with me. I burrowed through the dusty manuscripts as if I had a map to show me the way, and it was not long before I found what I had been seeking.

A few days later I returned the key to Msgr. Mercati and asked permission to return to Monte Cassino. He looked at my face and smiled. "I am glad you have found the Stream, my son," he said. "Now I hope you will find the Source."

And again he handed me a letter dated the day before, this time asking the Abbot to let me· use the large vitrines in the Scriptorium.

I delved into the archives of Monte Cassino like a fish returning to water. The River of St. Benedict carried me, the Stream of St. Jerome, which I had discovered in the precious repository in the locked room, urged me on, and I pored over unexpurgated editions of Josephus, Philo and Plinius, along with many other Latin classics. Again I looked through beautiful manuscripts of St. Jerome. Many of these priceless works had generally been considered long lost, and I read and read through a treasure-trove of unbelievable richness. I learned that other copies of his works survived in other Benedictine monasteries, such as the library of San Salvatore, where a beautiful copy remained for centuries until, with the destruction of the abbey, it reached the Biblioteca Laurenziana of Florence, where it is now classified as "the Amiatino Gospel."

The original manuscripts of St. Jerome, believed lost in the fifth century, fortunately survived in the Benedictine monastery of Monte Cassino and in the Secret Archives of the Vatican. Among these manuscripts was the complete text of the Essene Gospel of Peace.

I had found the Source: Hebrew fragments of the Essene Gospel, the Aramaic version of which I had just read from the shelves of Msgr. Mercati's locked room. I knew now the origin of the inner light that shone from that beloved figure, and I perceived in a flash of awareness the heroic measure of his silence. Now, should I be silent, too?

I returned to the Vatican and immediately went to Msgr. Mercati's office, that book-filled study I had come to know and love so well. When he looked up, I saw something new in his expression: mingled with his familiar glance of wise compassion was an indecipherable look almost of commiseration— of something shared that he had shared with no other person.

"You have found the Source," he said, quietly.

"How do you know?" I asked.

"Because, my son," he said, with a twinkle, "you have that look."

And again that strange expression crossed his face: I saw mirrored there all the wisdom and compassion of the ages, mingled with tender humor and the sharing of an unutterably precious secret. Tears suddenly stung my eyes.

"What shall I do, Father?" I asked. He did not have to ask what I was referring to.

"Let St. Francis sing in your heart," he whispered.

I knelt and kissed his hand. He said only one word, the shortest one-letter word, in Latin, *"I."* Go. And I went, and I never saw him again.

After more than half a century, certain memories grow dim and lose importance, while others, small incidents when they occurred, assume greater meaning in perspective. In the end, it is not the great discovery or the dramatic adventure that comes to mind when I remember Msgr. Mercati, but the shining moments of spiritual beauty, the unsullied nobility of his soul, exemplified in two small episodes.

One afternoon, not long after I had begun my studies at the Vatican, I went to his office to ask a question. I opened his door a crack, after knocking and receiving no answer. He was sitting at his desk, deep in meditation, his hands folded in prayer. Through the stained glass window, the colors of the sunset shone on his head. I stopped, just before his secretary captured me.

"Please do not disturb him," he said. "He is praying for the souls of Galileo and Giordano Bruno."

I was stunned by his words, and I left quietly to digest their meaning. Although young, I realized how rare was a man who worshipped truth even beyond the holy vows that bound him to his church.

The other episode I will never forget occurred at the end of September. I was in my roof-top abode, sitting on a wooden box that served as a table, just starting my dinner which consisted of a slice of black peasant bread, a small piece of goat cheese which I had bought from the tiny store in the neighborhood, and my most cherished possession, two beautiful peaches given to me by the Signora, who got them from her brother in Milano.

I was used to all kinds of exuberant noises coming from below, but this time the noise reached fever pitch, and I got up from my wooden box to investigate. Suddenly I saw the tall, slender figure of Msgr. Mercati emerging from the staircase. I could hardly believe my eyes, but it was really he, the world-renowned Prefect of the Archives of the Vatican, climbing up to my roof-top, followed by the sum total of the inhabitants of the house, all in great excitement. I have no idea what words I uttered as I invited him to sit down on my old box, but I do remember that I offered him the two peaches. Of course, within a minute, the Signora came with a whole bowl of beautiful peaches, offering them to the "Prince of the Church" as she called to her son to bring a chair. But he sat down good-naturedly on the wooden box and said to her gently, "No, my friend, I am not a prince, only a simple librarian, and please do not bother to bring me a chair. I only came to have a talk with my student." With unusual perception, they understood the discreet allusion, and reluctantly retired downstairs.

"You have a nice view here," he smiled, looking at my improvised shelter. "But in a few weeks the northern winds will blow away your palacio and you will freeze." As he finished one of the two peaches, he took an envelope from his pocket. He went on, "Msgr. Mondik, my dear friend, is sending to you this modest gift." Opening the envelope, I saw one hundred lira in it. "And," he continued, "I think you will need this also, my modest gift." Another hundred lira appeared in his hands. "Then you will be able to fix your abode to withstand the cold."

My face must have reflected my emotions, for he put his hand gently on my shoulder, saying, "Do not worry, my son, you will still keep your vow of poverty. You will just eat a little better, and the north wind will not blow you off the roof."

I started to thank him, but he stopped me with a bene-diction, the pious gesture of his hands accompanied by a merry twinkle in his eyes. Then he was gone, as swiftly and silently as he had come. The awestruck inhabitants of the house watched from every window until he turned the corner and was out of sight.

AND then many sick and maimed came to Jesus, asking him: "If you know all things, tell us, why do we suffer with these grievous plagues? Why are we not whole like other men? Master, heal us, that we too may be made strong, and need abide no longer in our misery. We know that you have it in your power to heal all manner of disease. Free us from Satan and from all his great afflictions. Master, have compassion on us."

And Jesus answered: "Happy are you, that you hunger for the truth, for I will satisfy you with the bread of wisdom. Happy are you, that you knock, for I will open to you the door of life. Happy are you, that you would cast off the power of Satan, for I will lead you into the kingdom of our Mother's angels, where the power of Satan cannot enter."

And they asked him in amazement: "Who is our Mother and which her angels? And where is her kingdom?"

"Your Mother is in you, and you in her. She bore you; she gives you life. It was she who gave to you your body, and to her shall you one day give it back again. Happy are you when you come to know her and her kingdom; if you receive your Mother's angels and if you do her laws. I tell you truly, he who does these things shall never see disease. For the power of our Mother is above all. And it destroys Satan and his kingdom, and has rule over all your bodies and all living things.

"The blood which runs in us is born of the blood of our Earthly Mother. Her blood falls from the clouds; leaps up from the womb of the earth; babbles in the brooks of the mountains; flows wide in the rivers of the plains; sleeps in the lakes; rages mightily in the tempestuous seas.

"The air which we breathe is born of the breath of our Earthly Mother. Her breath is azure in the heights of the heavens; soughs in the tops of the mountains; whispers in the leaves of the forest; billows over the cornfields; slumbers in the deep valleys; burns hot in the desert.

"The hardness of our bones is born of the bones of our Earthly Mother, of the rocks and of the stones. They stand naked to the heavens on the tops of mountains; are as giants that lie sleeping on the sides of the mountains, as idols set in the desert, and are hidden in the deepness of the earth.

"The tenderness of our flesh is born of the flesh of our Earthly Mother; whose flesh waxes yellow and red in the fruits of the trees, and nurtures us in the furrows of the fields.

"Our bowels are born of the bowels of our Earthly Mother, and are hid from our eyes, like the invisible depths of the earth.

"The light of our eyes, the hearing of our ears, both are born of the colours and the sounds of our Earthly Mother; which enclose us about, as the waves of the sea a fish, as the eddying air a bird.

"I tell you in very truth, Man is the Son of the Earthly Mother, and from her did the Son of Man receive his whole body, even as the body of the newborn babe is born of the womb of his mother. I tell you truly, you are one with the Earthly Mother; she is in you, and you in her. Of her were you born, in her do you live, and to her shall you return again. Keep, therefore, her laws, for none can live long, neither be happy, but he who honours his Earthly Mother and does her laws. For your breath is her breath; your blood her blood; your bone her bone; your flesh her flesh; your bowels her bowels; your eyes and your ears are her eyes and her ears.

"I tell you truly, should you fail to keep but one only of all these laws, should you harm but one only of all your body's members, you shall be utterly lost in your grievous sickness, and there shall be weeping and gnashing of teeth. I tell you, unless you follow the laws of your Mother, you can in no wise escape death. And he who clings to the laws of his Mother, to him shall his Mother cling also. She shall heal all his plagues, and he shall never become sick. She gives him long life, and protects him from all afflictions; from fire, from water, from the bite of venomous serpents. For your Mother bore you, keeps life within you. She has given you her body, and none but she heals you. Happy is he who loves his Mother and lies quietly in her bosom. For your Mother loves you, even when you turn away from her. And how much more shall she love you, if you turn to her again? I tell you truly, very great is her love, greater than the greatest of mountains, deeper than the deepest seas. And those who love their Mother, she never deserts them. As the hen protects her chickens, as the lioness her cubs, as the mother her newborn babe, so does the Earthly Mother protect the Son of Man from all danger and all evils.

"For I tell you truly, evils and dangers innumerable lie in wait for the Sons of Men. Beelzebub, the prince of all devils, the source of every evil, lies in wait in the body of all the Sons of Men. He is death, the lord of every plague, and taking upon him a pleasing raiment, he tempts and entices the Sons of Men. Riches does he promise, and power, and splendid palaces, and garments of gold and silver, and a multitude of servants, all these; he promises renown and glory, fornication and lustfulness, gluttony and winebibbing, riotous living, and slothfulness and idle days. And he entices every one by that to which their heart is most inclined. And in the day that the Sons of Men have already become the slaves of all these vanities and abominations, then in payment thereof he snatches from the Sons of Men all those things which the Earthly Mother gave them so abundantly. He takes from them their breath, their blood, their bone, their flesh, their bowels, their eyes and their ears.

"But if the erring Son of Man be sorry for his sins and undo them, and return again to his Earthly Mother; and if he do his Earthly Mother's laws and free himself from Satan's clutches, resisting his temptations, then does the Earthly Mother receive again her erring Son with love and sends him her angels that they may serve him. I tell you truly, when the Son of Man resists the Satan that dwells in him and does not his will, in the same hour are found the Mother's angels there, that they may serve him with all their power and free utterly the Son of Man from the power of Satan.

"For no man can serve two masters. For either he serves Beelzebub and his devils or else he serves our Earthly Mother and her angels. Either he serves death or he serves life. I tell you truly, happy are those that do the laws of life and wander not upon the paths of death. For in them the forces of life wax strong and they escape the plagues of death."

And all those round about him listened to his words with amazement, for his word was with power, and he taught quite otherwise than the priests and scribes.

And though the sun was now set, they departed not to their homes. They sat round about Jesus and asked him: "Master, which are these laws of life? Rest with us awhile longer and teach us. We would listen to your teaching that we may be healed and become righteous."

And Jesus himself sat down in their midst and said: "I tell you truly, none can be happy, except he do the law."

And the others answered: "We all do the laws of Moses, our lawgiver, even as they are written in the holy scriptures."

And Jesus answered: "Seek not the law in your scriptures, for the law is life, whereas the scripture is dead. I tell you truly, Moses received not his laws from God in writing, but through the living word. The law is living word of living God to living prophets for living men. In everything that is life is the law written. You find it in the grass, in the tree, in the river, in the mountain, in the birds of heaven, in the fishes of the sea; but seek it chiefly in yourselves. For I tell you truly, all living things are nearer to God than the scripture which is without life. God so made life and all living things that they might by the everliving word teach the laws of the true God to man. God wrote not the laws in the pages of books, but in your heart and in your spirit. They are in your breath, your blood, your bone; in your flesh, your bowels, your eyes, your ears, and in every little part of your body. They are present in the air, in the water, in the earth, in the plants, in the sunbeams, in the depths and in the heights. They all speak to you that you may understand the tongue and the will of the living God. But you shut your eyes that you may not see, and you shut your ears that you may not hear. I tell you truly, that the scripture is the work of man, but life and all its hosts are the work of our God. Wherefore do you not listen to the words of God which are written in His works? And wherefore do you study the dead scriptures which are the work of the hands of men?"

"How may we read the laws of God elsewhere than in the scriptures? Where are they written? Read them to us from there where you see them, for we know nothing else but the scriptures which we have inherited from our forefathers. Tell us the laws of which you speak, that hearing them we may be healed and justified."

Jesus said: "You do not understand the words of life, because you are in death. Darkness darkens your eyes and your ears are stopped with deafness. For I tell you, it profits you not at all that you pore over dead scriptures if by your deeds you deny him who has given you the scriptures. I tell you truly, God and his laws are not in that which you do. They are not in gluttony and in winebibbing, neither in riotous living, nor in lustfulness, nor in seeking after riches, nor yet in hatred of your enemies. For all these things are far from the true God and from his angels. But all these things come from the kingdom of darkness and the lord of all evils. And all these things do you carry in yourselves; and so the word and the power of God enter not into you, because all manner of evil and all manner of abominations have their dwelling in your body and your spirit. If you will that the living God's word and his power may enter you, defile not your body and your spirit; for the body is the temple of the spirit, and the spirit is the temple of God. Purify, therefore, the temple, that the Lord of the temple may dwell therein and occupy a place that is worthy of him.

"And from all temptations of your body and your spirit, coming from Satan, withdraw beneath the shadow of God's heaven.

"Renew yourselves and fast. For I tell you truly, that Satan and his plagues may only be cast out by fasting and by prayer. Go by yourself and fast alone, and show your fasting to no man. The living God shall see it and great shall be your reward. And fast till Beelzebub and all his evils depart from you, and all the angels of our Earthly Mother come and serve you. For I tell you truly, except you fast, you shall never be freed from the power of Satan and from all diseases that come from Satan. Fast and pray fervently, seeking the power of the living God for your healing. While you fast, eschew the Sons of Men and seek our Earthly Mother's angels, for he that seeks shall find.

"Seek the fresh air of the forest and of the fields, and there in the midst of them shall you find the angel of air. Put off your shoes and your clothing and suffer the angel of air to embrace all your body. Then breathe long and deeply, that the angel of air may be brought within you. I tell you truly, the angel of air shall cast out of your body all uncleannesses which defiled it without and within. And thus shall all evil-smelling and unclean things rise out of you, as the smoke of fire curls upwards and is lost in the sea of the air. For I tell you truly, holy is the angel of air, who cleanses all that is unclean and makes all evil-smelling things of a sweet odour. No man may come before the face of God, whom the angel of air lets not pass. Truly, all must be born again by air and by truth, for your body breathes the air of the Earthly Mother, and your spirit breathes the truth of the Heavenly Father.

"After the angel of air, seek the angel of water. Put off your shoes and your clothing and suffer the angel of water to embrace all your body. Cast yourselves wholly into his enfolding arms, and as often as you move the air with your breath, move with your body the water also. I tell you truly, the angel of water shall cast out of your body all uncleannesses which defiled it without and within. And all unclean and evil-smelling things shall flow out of you, even as the uncleannesses of garments washed in water flow away and are lost in the stream of the river. I tell you truly, holy is the angel of water who cleanses all that is unclean and makes all evil-smelling things of a sweet odour. No man may come before the face of God, whom the angel of water lets not pass. In very truth, all must be born again of water and of truth, for your body bathes in the river of earthly life, and your spirit bathes in the river of life everlasting. For you receive your blood from our Earthly Mother and the truth from our Heavenly Father.

"And if afterward there remain within you aught of your past sins and uncleannesses, seek the angel of sunlight. Put off your shoes and your clothing and suffer the angel of sunlight to embrace all your body. Then breathe long and deeply, that the angel of sunlight may be brought within you. And the angel of sunlight shall cast out of your body all evil-smelling and unclean things which defiled it without and within. And all unclean and evil-smelling things shall rise from you, even as the darkness of night fades before the brightness of the rising sun. For I tell you truly, holy is the angel of

sunlight who cleans out all uncleannesses and makes all evil-smelling things of a sweet odour. None may come before the face of God, whom the angel of sunlight lets not pass. Truly, all must be born again of sun and of truth, for your body basks in the sunlight of the Earthly Mother, and your spirit basks in the sunlight of truth of the Heavenly Father.

"The angels of air and of water and of sunlight are brethren. They were given to the Son of Man that they might serve him, and that he might go always from one to the other.

"Holy, likewise, is their embrace. They are indivisible children of the Earthly Mother, so do not you put asunder those whom earth and heaven have made one. Let these three brother angels enfold you every day and let them abide with you through all your fasting.

It was said to you: 'Honour thy father and thy mother that thy days may be long upon this earth.' But I say to you, Sons of Man: Honour your Earthly Mother and keep all her laws, that your days may be long on this earth, and honour your Heavenly Father that eternal life may be yours in the heavens. For the Heavenly Father is a hundred times greater than all fathers by seed and by blood, and greater is the Heavenly Mother than all mothers by the body. And dearer is the Son of Man in the eyes of his Heavenly Father and of his Earthly Mother than are children in the eyes of their fathers by seed and by blood and of their mothers by the body. And more wise are the words and laws of your Heavenly Father and of your Earthly Mother than the words and the will of all fathers by seed and by blood, and of all mothers by the body. And of more worth also is the inheritance of your Heavenly Father and of your Earthly Mother, the everlasting kingdom of earthly and heavenly life, than all the inheritances of your fathers by seed and by blood, and of your mothers by the body.

"And your true brothers are all those who do the will of your Heavenly Father and of your Earthly Mother, and not your brothers by blood. I tell you truly, that your true brothers in the will of the Heavenly Father and of the Earthly Mother will love you a thousand times more than your brothers by blood. For since the days of Cain and Abel, when brothers by blood transgressed the will of God, there is no true brotherhood by blood. And brothers do unto brothers as do strangers. Therefore, I say to you, love your true brothers in the will of God a thousand times more than your brothers by blood.

"FOR YOUR HEAVENLY FATHER IS LOVE.
"FOR YOUR EARTHLY MOTHER IS LOVE.
"FOR THE SON OF MAN IS LOVE.

"It is by love that the Heavenly Father and the Earthly Mother and the Son of Man become one. For the spirit of the Son of Man was created from the spirit of the Heavenly Father, and his body from the body of the Earthly Mother. Become, therefore, perfect as the spirit of your Heavenly Father and the body of your Earthly Mother are perfect. And so love your Heavenly Father, as he loves your spirit. And so love your Earthly Mother, as she loves your body. And so love your true brothers, as your Heavenly Father and your Earthly Mother love them. And then your Heavenly Father shall give you his holy spirit, and your Earthly Mother shall give you her holy body. And then shall the Sons of Men like true brothers give love one to another, the love which they received from their Heavenly Father and from their Earthly Mother; and they shall all become comforters one of another. And then shall disappear from the earth all evil and all sorrow, and there shall be love and joy upon earth. And then shall the earth be like the heavens, and the kingdom of God shall come. And then shall come the Son of Man in all his glory, to inherit the kingdom of God. And then shall the Sons of Men divide their divine inheritance, the kingdom of God. For the Sons of Man live in the Heavenly Father and in the Earthly Mother, and the Heavenly Father and the Earthly Mother live in them. And then with the kingdom of God shall come the end of the times. For the Heavenly Father's love gives to all life everlasting in the kingdom of God. For love is eternal. Love is stronger than death.

"And now I speak to you in the living tongue of the living God, through the holy spirit of our Heavenly Father. There is none yet among you that can understand all of this which I speak. He who expounds to you the scriptures speaks to you in a dead tongue of dead men, through his diseased and mortal body. Him, therefore, can all men understand, for all men are diseased and all are in death. No one sees the light of life. Blind man leads blind on the dark paths of sins, diseases and sufferings; and at the last all fall into the pit of death.

"I am sent to you by the Father, that I may make the light of life to shine before you. The light lightens itself and the darkness, but the darkness knows only itself, and knows not the light. I have still many things to say to you, but you cannot bear them yet. For your eyes are used to the darkness, and the full light of the Heavenly Father would make you blind. Therefore, you cannot yet understand that which I speak to you concerning the Heavenly Father who sent me to you. Follow, therefore, first, only the laws of your Earthly Mother, of which I have told you. And when her angels shall have cleansed and renewed your bodies and strengthened your eyes, you will be able to bear the light of our Heavenly Father. When you can gaze on the brightness of the noonday sun with unflinching eyes, you can then look upon the blinding light of your Heavenly Father, which is a thousand times brighter than the brightness of a thousand suns. But how should you look upon the blinding light of your Heavenly Father, when you cannot even bear the shining of the blazing sun? Believe me, the sun is as the flame of a candle beside the sun of truth of the Heavenly Father. Have but faith, therefore, and hope, and love. I tell you truly, you shall not want your reward. If you believe in my words, you believe in him who sent me, who is the lord of all, and with whom all things are possible. For what is impossible with men, all these things are possible with God. If you believe in the angels of the Earthly Mother and do her laws, your faith shall sustain you and you shall never see disease. Have hope also in the love of your Heavenly Father, for he who trusts in him shall never be deceived, nor shall he ever see death.

"Love one another, for God is love, and so shall his angels know that you walk in his paths. And then shall all the angels come before your face and serve you. And Satan with all sins, diseases and uncleannesses shall depart from your body. Go, eschew your sins; repent yourselves; baptise yourselves; that

you may be born again and sin no more."

Then Jesus rose. But all else remained sitting, for every man felt the power of his words. And then the full moon appeared between the breaking clouds and folded Jesus in its brightness. And sparks flew upward from his hair, and he stood among them in the moonlight, as though he hovered in the air. And no man moved, neither was the voice of any heard. And no one knew how long a time had passed, for time stood still.

Then Jesus stretched out his hands to them and said: "Peace be with you." And so he departed, as a breath of wind sways the green of trees.

And for a long while yet the company sat still and then they woke in the silence, one man after another, like as from a long dream. But none would go, as if the words of him who had left them ever sounded in their ears. And they sat as though they listened to some wondrous music.

But at last one, as it were a little fearfully, said: "How good it is to be here." Another: "Would that this night were everlasting." And others: "Would that he might be with us always." "Of a truth he is God's messenger, for he planted hope within our hearts." And no man wished to go home, saying: "I go not home where all is dark and joyless. Why should we go home where no one loves us?"

And they spoke on this wise, for they were almost all poor, lame, blind, maimed, beggars, homeless, despised in their wretchedness, who were only borne for pity's sake in the houses where they found a few days' refuge. Even certain, who had both home and family, said: "We also will stay with you." For every man felt that the words of him who was gone bound the little company with threads invisible.

74

And all felt that they were born again. They saw before them a shining world, even when the moon was hidden in the clouds. And in the hearts of all blossomed wondrous flowers of wondrous beauty, the flowers of joy.

And when the bright sunbeams appeared over the earth's rim, they all felt that it was the sun of the coming kingdom of God. And with joyful countenances they went forth to meet God's angels.

———

And it was by the bed of a stream, many sick fasted and prayed with God's angels for seven days and seven nights. And great was their reward, because they followed Jesus' words. And with the passing of the seventh day, all their pains left them. And when the sun rose over the earth's rim they saw Jesus coming towards them from the mountain, with the brightness of the rising sun about his head.

"Peace be with you."

And they said no word at all, but only cast themselves down before him, and touched the hem of his garment in token of their healing.

"Give thanks not to me, but to your Earthly Mother, who sent you her healing angels. Go, and sin no more, that you may never again see disease. And let the healing angels become your guardians."

But they answered him: "Whither should we go, Master, for with you are the words of eternal life? Tell us, what are the sins which we must shun, that we may nevermore see disease?"

Jesus answered: "Be it so according to your faith," and he sat down among them, saying:

"It was said to them of old time, 'Honour thy Heavenly Father and thy Earthly Mother, and do their commandments, that thy days may be long upon the earth.' And next afterward was given this commandment, 'Thou shalt not kill,' for life is given to all by God, and that which God has given, let not man take away. For I tell you truly, from one Mother proceeds all that lives upon the earth. Therefore, he who kills, kills his brother. And from him will the Earthly Mother turn away, and will pluck from him her quickening breasts. And he will be shunned by her angels, and Satan will have his dwelling in his body. And the flesh of slain beasts in his body will become his own tomb. For I tell you truly, he who kills, kills himself, and whoso eats the flesh of slain beasts, eats of the body of death. For in his blood every drop of their blood turns to poison; in his breath their breath to stink; in his flesh their flesh to boils; in his bones their bones to chalk; in his bowels their bowels to decay; in his eyes their eyes to scales; in his ears their ears to waxy issue. And their death will become his death. For only in the service of your Heavenly Father are your debts of seven years forgiven in seven days. But Satan forgives you nothing and you must pay him for all. 'Eye for eye, tooth for tooth, hand for hand, foot for foot; burning for burning; wound for wound;' life for life, death for death. For the wages of sin is death. Kill not, neither eat the flesh of your innocent prey, lest you become the slaves of Satan. For that is the path of sufferings, and it leads unto death. But do the will of God, that his angels may serve you on the way of life. Obey, therefore, the words of God: 'Behold, I have given you every herb bearing seed, which is upon the face of all the earth, and every tree, in the which is the fruit of a tree yielding seed; to you it shall be for

76

meat. And to every beast of the earth, and to every fowl of the air, and to everything that creepeth upon the earth, wherein there is breath of life, I give every green herb for meat. Also the milk of every thing that moveth and that liveth upon earth shall be meat for you; even as the green herb have I given unto them, so I give their milk unto you. But flesh, and the blood which quickens it, shall ye not eat.

For I tell you truly, man is more than the beast. But he who kills a beast without a cause, though the beast attack him not, through lust for slaughter, or for its flesh, or for its hide, or yet for its tusks, evil is the deed which he does, for he is turned into a wild beast himself. Wherefore is his end also as the end of the wild beasts."

"And when you come before the face of God, his angels bear witness for you with your good deeds. And God sees your good deeds written in your bodies and in your spirits, and rejoices in his heart. He blesses your body and your spirit and all your deeds, and gives you for a heritage his earthly and heavenly kingdom, that in it you may have life everlasting. Happy is he who can enter into the kingdom of God, for he shall never see death."

Then another said: "Moses, the greatest in Israel, suffered our forefathers to eat the flesh of clean beasts, and forbade only the flesh of unclean beasts. Why, therefore, do you forbid us the flesh of all beasts? Which law comes from God? That of Moses or your law?"

And Jesus answered: "God gave, by Moses, ten commandments to your forefathers. These commandments are hard,' said your forefathers, and could not keep them. When Moses saw this, he had compassion on his people, and would not that they perish. And then he gave them ten times ten commandments, less hard, that· they might follow them. I tell you truly, if your forefathers had been able to keep the ten commandments of God, Moses would never had need of his ten times ten commandments. For he whose feet are strong as the mountain of Zion, needs no crutches; but he whose limbs do shake, gets further having crutches, than without them. And Moses said to the Lord: 'My heart is filled with sorrow, for my people will be lost. For they are without knowledge, and are not able to understand thy commandments. They are as little children who cannot yet understand their father's words. Suffer, Lord, that I give them other laws, that they may not perish. If they may not be with thee, Lord, let them not be against thee; that they may sustain themselves, and when the time has come, and they are ripe for thy words, reveal to them thy laws.' For that did Moses break the two tablets of stone whereon were written the ten commandments, and he gave them ten times ten in their stead. And of these ten times ten the Scribes and Pharisees have made a hundred times ten commandments. And they have laid unbearable burdens on your shoulders, that they themselves do not carry. For the more nigh are the commandments to God, the less do we need; and the farther they are from God, then the more do we need. Wherefore are the laws of the Pharisees and Scribes innumerable; the laws of the Son of Man seven; of the angels three; and of God one.

"Therefore, I teach you only those laws which you can understand, that you may become men, and follow the seven laws of the Son of Man. Then will the angels also reveal their laws to you, that God's holy spirit may descend upon you, and lead you to his law."

And all were astonished at his wisdom, and asked him: "Continue, Master, and teach us all the laws which we can receive."

And Jesus continued: "God commanded your forefathers: 'Thou shalt not kill.' But their heart was hardened and they killed. Then Moses desired that at least they should not kill men, and he suffered them to kill beasts. And then the heart of your forefathers was hardened yet more, and they killed men and beasts likewise. But I do say to you: Kill neither men, nor beasts, nor yet the food which goes into your mouth. For if you eat living food, the same will quicken you, but if you kill your food, the dead food will kill you also. For life comes only from life, and from death comes always death. For everything which kills your foods, kills your bodies also. And everything which kills your bodies kills your souls also. And your bodies become what your foods are, even as your spirits, likewise, become what your thoughts are. You shall live only by the fire of life, and prepare not your foods with the fire of death, which kills your foods, your bodies and your souls also."

"Master, where is the fire of life?" asked some of them.

"In you, in your blood and in your bodies."

"And the fire of death?" asked others.

"It is the fire which blazes outside your body, which is hotter than your blood. With that fire of death you cook your foods in your homes and in your fields. I tell you truly, it is the same fire which destroys your foods and your bodies, even as the fire of malice, which ravages your thoughts, ravages your spirits. For your body is that which you eat, and your spirit is that which you think. Eat nothing, therefore, which a stronger fire than the fire of life has killed. Wherefore, prepare and eat all fruits of trees, and all grasses of the fields, and all milk of beasts good for eating. For all these are fed and ripened by the fire of life; all are the gift of the angels of our Earthly Mother. But eat nothing to which only the fire of death gives savour, for such is of Satan."

"How should we cook our daily bread without fire, Master?" asked some with great astonishment.

"Let the angels of God prepare your bread. Moisten your wheat, that the angel of water may enter it. Then set it in the air, that the angel of air also may embrace it. And leave it from morning to evening beneath the sun, that the angel of sunshine may descend upon it. And the blessing of the three angels will soon make the germ of life to sprout in your wheat.   For the angels of water, of air, and of sunshine fed and ripened the wheat in the field, and they, likewise, must prepare also your bread. And the same sun which, with the fire of life, made the wheat to grow and ripen, must cook your bread with the same fire. For the fire of the sun gives life to the wheat, to the bread, and to the body. But the fire of death kills the wheat, the bread, and the body. And the living angels of the living God serve only living men. For God is the God of the living, and not the God of the dead.

"So eat always from the table of God: the fruits of the trees, the grain and grasses of the field, the milk of beasts, and the honey of bees. For everything beyond these is of Satan, and leads by the way of sins and of diseases unto death. But the foods which you eat from the abundant table of God give strength and youth to your body, and you will never see disease. For the table of God fed Methuselah of old, and I tell you truly, if you live even as he lived, then will the God of the living give you also long life upon the earth as was his.

"For I tell you truly, the God of the living is richer than all the rich of the earth, and his abundant table is richer than the richest table of feasting of all the rich upon the earth. Eat, therefore, all your life at the table of our Earthly Mother, and you will never see want. And when you eat at her table, eat all things even as they are found on the table of the Earthly Mother. Cook not, neither mix all things one with another, lest your bowels become as steaming bogs. For I tell you truly, this is abominable in the eyes of the Lord.

"Take heed, therefore, and defile not with all kinds of abominations the temple of your bodies. Be content with two or three sorts of food, which you will find always upon the table of our Earthly Mother. And desire not to devour all things which you see round about you. For I tell you truly, if you mix together all sorts of food in your body, then the peace of your body will cease, and endless war will rage in you. And it will be blotted out even as homes and kingdoms divided against themselves work their own destruction. For your God is the God of peace, and does never help division. Arouse not, therefore, against you the wrath of God, lest he drive you from his table, and lest you be compelled to go to the table of Satan, where the fire of sins, of diseases, and of death will corrupt your body."

"And when you eat, never eat unto fulness. Flee the temptations of Satan, and listen to the voice of

God's angels. For Satan and his power tempt you
always to eat more and more. But live by the spirit,
and resist the desires of the body. And your fasting
is always pleasing in the eyes of the angels of God.
So give heed to how much you have eaten when
your body is sated, and always eat less by a third.
Then will the angels of God serve you always, and
you will never fall into the bondage of Satan and of
his diseases. Trouble not the work of the angels in
your body by eating often. For I tell you truly, he
who eats more than twice in the day does in him the
work of Satan. And the angels of God leave his
body, and soon Satan will take possession of it.
Eat only when the sun is highest in the heavens, and
again when it is set. And you will never see disease,
for such finds favour in the eyes of the Lord. The
angels will rejoice in your body, and your days
will be long upon the earth, for this is pleasing in
the eyes of the Lord. Eat always when the table of
God is served before you, and eat always of that
which you find upon the table of God. For I tell
you truly, God knows well what your body needs,
and when it needs.

"Happy and wise are they that eat only at the
table of God, and eschew all the abominations of
Satan. Eat not unclean foods brought from far
countries, but eat always that which your trees bear.
For your God knows well what is needful for you,
and where and when. And he gives to all peoples of
all kingdoms for food that which is best for each.
Eat not as the heathen do, who stuff themselves in
haste, defiling their bodies with all manner of abominations.

"For the power of God's angels enters into you
with the living food which the Lord gives you from

his royal table. And when you eat, have above you the angel of air, and below you the angel of water. Breathe long and deeply at all your meals, that the angel of air may bless your repasts. And chew well your food with your teeth, that it become water, and that the angel of water turn it into blood in your body. And eat slowly, as it were a prayer you make to the Lord. For I tell you truly, the power of God enters into you, if you eat after this manner at his table. For the table of the Lord is as an altar, and he who eats at the table of God, is in a temple. For I tell you truly, the body of the Sons of Man is turned into a temple, and their inwards into an altar, if they do the commandments of God. Wherefore, put naught upon the altar of the Lord when your spirit is vexed, neither think upon any one with anger in the temple of God. And enter only into the Lord's sanctuary when you feel in yourselves the call of his angels, for all that you eat in sorrow, or in anger, or without desire, becomes a poison in your body. For the breath of Satan defiles all these. Place with joy your offerings upon the altar of your body, and let all evil thoughts depart from you when you receive into your body the power of God from his table. And never sit at the table of God before he call you by the angel of appetite.

"Rejoice, therefore, always with God's angels at their royal table, for this is pleasing to the heart of the Lord. And your life will be long upon the earth, for the most precious of God's servants will serve you all your days: the angel of joy.

"And forget not that every seventh day is holy and consecrated to God. On six days feed your body with the gifts of the Earthly Mother, but on the seventh day sanctify your body for your Heavenly

Father. And on the seventh day eat not any earthly food, but live only upon the words of God. And be all the day with the angels of the Lord in the kingdom of the Heavenly Father. And on the seventh day let the angels of God build the kingdom of the heavens in your body, as you labour for six days in the kingdom of the Earthly Mother. And let not food trouble the work of the angels in your body throughout the seventh day. And God will give you long life upon earth, that you may have life everlasting in the kingdom of the heavens. For I tell you truly, if you see not diseases any more upon the earth, you will live for ever in the kingdom of the heavens.

"And God will send you each morning the angel of sunshine to wake you from your sleep. Therefore, obey your Heavenly Father's summons, and lie not idle in your beds, for the angels of air and water await you already without. And labour all day long with the angels of the Earthly Mother that you may come to know them and their works ever more and more well. But when the sun is set, and your Heavenly Father sends you his most precious angel, sleep, then take your rest, and be all the night with the angel of sleep. And then will your Heavenly Father send you his unknown angels, that they may be with you the livelong night. And the Heavenly Father's unknown angels will teach you many things concerning the kingdom of God, even as the angels that you know of the Earthly Mother, instruct you in the things of her kingdom. For I tell you truly, you will be every night the guests of the kingdom of your Heavenly Father, if you do his commandments. And when you wake up upon the morrow, you will feel in you the power of the unknown angels. And your Heavenly Father will send them to

85

you every night, that they may build your spirit, even as every day the Earthly Mother sends you her angels, that they may build your body. For I tell you truly, if in the daytime your Earthly Mother folds you in her arms, and in the night the Heavenly Father breathes his kiss upon you, then will the Sons of Men become the Sons of God.

"Shun all that is too hot and too cold. For it is the will of your Earthly Mother that neither heat nor cold should harm your body. And let not your bodies become either hotter or colder than as God's angels warm or cool them. And if you do the commandments of the Earthly Mother, then as oft as your body becomes too hot, will she send the angel of coolness to cool you, and as oft as your body becomes too cold, will she send you the angel of heat to warm you again.

"Follow the example of all the angels of the Heavenly Father and of the Earthly Mother, who work day and night, without ceasing, upon the kingdoms of the heavens and of the earth. Therefore, receive also into yourselves the strongest of God's angels, the angel of deeds, and work all together upon the kingdom of God. Follow the example of the running water, the wind as it blows, the rising and setting of the sun, the growing plants and trees, the beasts as they run and gambol, the wane and waxing of the moon, the stars as they come and go again; all these do move, and do perform their labours. For all which has life does move, and only that which is dead is still. And God is the God of the living, and Satan that of the dead. Serve, therefore, the living God, that the eternal movement of life may sustain you, and that you may escape the eternal stillness of death. Work, therefore, without ceasing, to build the kingdom of God, lest you be cast into the kingdom of Satan. For eternal joy abounds in the living kingdom of God, but still sorrow darkens the kingdom of death of Satan. Be, therefore, true Sons of your Earthly Mother and of your Heavenly Father, that you fall not as slaves of Satan. And your Earthly Mother and Heavenly Father will send you their angels to teach, to love, and to serve you. And their angels will write the commandments of God in your head, in your heart, and in your hands, that you may know, feel, and do God's commandments.

"And pray every day to your Heavenly Father and Earthly Mother, that your soul become as perfect as your Heavenly Father's holy spirit is perfect, and that your body become as perfect as the body of your Earthly Mother is perfect. For if you understand, feel, and do the commandments, then all for which you pray to your Heavenly Father and your Earthly Mother will be given you. For the wisdom, the love, and the power of God are above all.

"After this manner, therefore, pray to your Heavenly Father: Our Father which art in heaven, hallowed be thy name. Thy kingdom come. Thy will be done on earth as it is in heaven. Give us this day our daily bread. And forgive us our debts, as we forgive our debtors. And lead us not into temptation, but deliver us from evil. For thine is the kingdom, the power, and the glory, for ever. Amen.

"And after this manner pray to your Earthly Mother: Our Mother which art upon earth, hallowed be thy name. Thy kingdom come, and thy will be done in us, as it is in thee. As thou sendest every day thy angels, send them to us also. Forgive us our sins, as we atone all our sins against thee. And lead us not into sickness, but deliver us from all evil, for thine is the earth, the body, and the health. Amen."

And they all prayed together with Jesus to the Heavenly Father and to the Earthly Mother.

And afterwards Jesus spoke thus to them: "Even as your bodies have been reborn through the Earthly Mother's angels, may your spirit, likewise, be reborn through the angels of the Heavenly Father. Become, therefore, true Sons of your Father and of your Mother, and true Brothers of the Sons of Men. Till now you were at war with your Father, with your Mother, and with your Brothers. And you have served Satan. From to-day live at peace with your Heavenly Father, and with your Earthly Mother, and with your Brothers, the Sons of Men. And fight only against Satan, lest he rob you of your peace. I give the peace of your Earthly Mother to your body, and the peace of your Heavenly Father to your spirit. And let the peace of both reign among the Sons of Men.

"Come to me all that are weary, and that suffer in strife and affliction! For my peace will strengthen you and comfort you. For my peace is exceeding full of joy. Wherefore do I always greet you after this manner: 'Peace be with you!' Do you always, therefore, so greet one another, that upon your body may descend the peace of your Earthly Mother, and upon your spirit the peace of your Heavenly Father. And then will you find peace also among yourselves, for the kingdom of God is within you. And now return to your Brothers with whom hitherto you were at war, and give your peace to them also. For happy are they that strive for peace, for they will find the peace of God. Go, and sin no

more. And give to every one your peace, even as I have given my peace unto you. For my peace is of God Peace be with you."

And he left them.

And his peace descended upon them; and in their heart the angel of love, in their head the wisdom of law, and in their hands the power of rebirth, they went forth among the Sons of Men, to bring the light of peace to those that warred in darkness.

And they parted, wishing, one to another:

"PEACE BE WITH YOU."

CREDO
of the International Biogenic Society

We believe that our most precious possession is Life.

We believe we shall mobilize all the forces of Life against the forces of death.

We believe that mutual understanding leads toward mutual cooperation; that mutual cooperation leads toward Peace; and that Peace is the only way of survival for mankind.

We believe that we shall preserve instead of waste our natural resources, which are the heritage of our children.

We believe that we shall avoid the pollution of our air, water, and soil, the basic preconditions of Life.

We believe we shall preserve the vegetation of our planet: the humble grass which came fifty million years ago, and the majestic trees which came twenty million years ago, to prepare our planet for mankind.

We believe we shall eat only fresh, natural, pure, whole foods, without chemicals and artificial processing.

We believe we shall live a simple, natural, creative life, absorbing all the sources of energy, harmony and knowledge.

We believe that the improvement of life and mankind on our planet must start with individual efforts, as the whole depends on the atoms composing it.

We believe in the Fatherhood of God, the Motherhood of Nature, and the Brotherhood of Man.

—composed in Paris in 1928 by Romain Rolland
and Edmond Bordeaux Székely

AN INVITATION
to the I.B.S. International Center in Costa Rica

Over the years, thousands upon thousands of truth-seekers from all over the world have written to us, asking for the opportunity to study and put into practice the Essene Biogenic teachings in a harmonious framework, in the company of those motivated by similar ideas and ideals. In response to this need, the International Biogenic Society, in cooperation with Norma Nilsson Bordeaux, successor of Edmond Bordeaux Szekely, conducts every summer and winter *International Seminars* on *The Essene Way and Biogenic Living,* attended by members, students and teachers from all over the world.

The Seminars take place at the beautiful International Center of the I.B.S. in Costa Rica, where seminar participants study the ageless truths of the Essene Way of Biogenic Living from a semi-outdoor lecture hall overlooking seven mountains and four rivers, with the legendary volcanic peaks of Irazu and Turrialba towering in the distance, surrounded by lush green vegetation and the scent of tropical flowers. But physical beauty is not the only reason for the choice of Costa Rica as the site of the International Center of the I.B.S. As those who have read Edmond Bordeaux Szekely's *The Greatness in the Smallness** know, Costa Rica is the home of the World University of Peace—where pacifism is a way of life, where there is no army nor manufacture of arms, an oasis of democracy and enlightened freedom in an increasingly troubled world.

If you would like to receive the announcement and program of the *International Seminars on The Essene Way and Biogenic Living,* please write to **I.B.S. Internacional, Apartado 372, Cartago, Costa Rica, Central America,** by *Air Mail only.*

*available from the above address for $7.50, plus 10% postage and handling.

RECOMMENDED BOOKS FOR STUDY

Many members who cannot attend the International Seminars because of distance or limited means are interested in a systematic program of home study. The following books are recommended for such a program, and provide an excellent foundation for study of *The Essene Way and Biogenic Living*, especially when coordinated with the methods outlined in *The Art of Study: the Sorbonne Method*. Also, it is recommended that these books be read and studied before attending the *International Seminars on The Essene Way and Biogenic Living*, held every year at the I.B.S. International Correspondence Center in Orosi, Costa Rica.

Please send me the following books:

_____*The Essene Gospel of Peace, Book One* $1.00

_____*The Essene Gospel of Peace, Book Two* $5.80

_____*The Essene Gospel of Peace, Book Three* $5.60

_____*The Essene Gospel of Peace, Book Four* $4.50

_____*The Essene Way—Biogenic Living* $8.80

_____*The Chemistry of Youth* $7.50

_____*From Enoch to the Dead Sea Scrolls* $4.80

_____*The Essene Code of Life* $3.50

_____*The Essene Science of Life* $3.50

_____*Archeosophy, a New Science* $4.80

_____*Books, Our Eternal Companions* $3.50

_____*Cosmos, Man and Society* $5.80

_____*Search for the Ageless, Volume I* $7.80

_____*The Ecological Health Garden, the Book of Survival* $4.50

_____*The Book of Living Foods* $3.50

_____*The Greatness in the Smallness* $7.50

_____*The Art of Study: the Sorbonne Method* $3.50

_____*Total*

_____*Add 10% for Postage & Handling*

_____*Total Amount Enclosed*

Please address all orders (by Air Mail) to:
I.B.S. INTERNACIONAL
Apartado 372, Cartago, Costa Rica, Central America

*Name*_____

*Address*_____

*City*_____*State*_____*Zip*_____

IMPORTANT ORDERING INFORMATION

All orders must be prepaid. Be sure to use Air Mail only. Minimum order: $5.00, minimum postage: 75¢. Please make Cashier's Check or Money Order in U.S. currency (payable on a U.S. bank) out to *I.B.S. Internacional.* Allow four weeks for processing. Members of the International Biogenic Society may deduct 20% and *active* Teachers of Biogenic Living may deduct 40% (both must have valid membership cards for the current year). Dealers and distributors, please write to above address for discount information. All sales are considered final.

APPLICATION FOR ASSOCIATE MEMBERSHIP
INTERNATIONAL BIOGENIC SOCIETY

Please return to: *I.B.S. INTERNACIONAL*
Apartado 372, Cartago
Costa Rica, Central America

*Date*_____

*Name*_____

*Address*_____

*City*_____*State*_____*Zip*_____

*Age*_____*Profession*_____

*Previous Experience*_____

*I am interested in*____*becoming an Associate Member of the I.B.S.*
____*becoming a Teacher of Biogenic Living.*

Enclosed is my annual Associate Membership fee of $20.00. Please mail my membership card, your next issue of the Periodical Review, and my copy of *The Essene Way—Biogenic Living*, my most important textbook and encyclopedia of ancient wisdom and modern practice. I understand I will receive a 20% discount on all publications as an Associate Member, but only if I order *directly* from I.B.S. Internacional.

Please make your check in U.S. currency out to
I.B.S. INTERNACIONAL

Please use *Air Mail* only.

The International Biogenic Society announces with pride
the publication of

THE FIRST ESSENE

In July 1979, I.B.S. members and teachers from all over the world gathered at the beautiful International Center of the I.B.S. in Orosi, Costa Rica, for the first *International Seminar on The Essene Way and Biogenic Living* to be held in Costa Rica. Everyone agreed it was the finest Seminar ever given by the founder of the International Biogenic Society, Dr. Edmond Bordeaux Szekely. What no one knew at the time was that it was also his last. Two weeks after the close of the last session, Dr. Szekely passed away, and thus the material he imparted during those six days became even more precious. Now the entire transcript of the Seminar is available in book form.

Shining from every page of *The First Essene* is the warmth, the laughter, the essential oneness with all humanity that was one of the most memorable qualities of Edmond Bordeaux Szekely. Profusely illustrated, it is as well a spiritual banquet. The most profound teachings of mankind are imparted in a clear and lucid way that is both easy to understand, and a lifetime challenge to put into practice. Watch the Creation take place on the Tapestry of the Universe; play the precolumbian Sacred Cosmic Ball Game; see how delicious "Zarathustra" bread is made from an 8000-year-old recipe—all in *The First Essene*, now available from I.B.S. Internacional. $9.50

Please order from *I.B.S. Internacional, Apartado 372, Cartago, Costa Rica, Central America.* Please use Air Mail and add 10% for postage and handling.